The Real Deal®

Volume 1

For Smart Car Buyers

How to Negotiate Like The Professionals!

Linda F. Balk

The Real Deal ®
Volume 1
For Smart Car Buyers

ISBN-13: 978-1495943669
ISBN-10: 1495943666

Library of Congress Control Number: 2014905523

Limits of Liability/Disclaimer of Warranty

Dedication

This book is dedicated to our parents and grandparents. Our grandparents lived through the great depression in the early 1900's and passed down stories of how the families managed to survive. There was little money, but they found ways to feed the family and take care of everyone. My parents, mindful of the lean times they had as children and young adults, passed down principles of frugal living that have helped our generation to prepare for good times and bad, always mindful that things can change in ways that cannot be anticipated. We will continue their heritage and will always be grateful.

Why You Have to Read

The Real Deal®
For Smart Car Buyers

The Real Deal® series is a gold mine for anyone who needs to solve real world financial problems! Amazing ways are revealed to negotiate on big ticket items and uncover hidden charges you probably didn't know about.

Have you ever felt intimidated when buying a car or any major purchase? Did you ever wonder if you might have paid too much?

Unfortunately, negotiation techniques are not a high priority in our educational system even though they may be more important than many of subjects included in the curriculum. Excellent students have gone all the way through high school and college without having any idea how to negotiate for anything.

All the practical tools are gathered together in this simple analysis of how to get The Real Deal® no matter what you are buying. Welcome to a new world of successful negotiation!

Table of Contents

Chapter 1: Introduction To The Real Deal®
For Smart Car Buyers………..1

Chapter 2: Arriving At The Showroom…..7

Chapter 3: The Second You Arrive
Negotiations Have Begun...........9

Chapter 4: Entering The Showroom……...13

Chapter 5: How You Can Get Ready In
Advance…………………....15

Chapter 6: New Car Versus Used………...19

Chapter 7: What Is The Price?................. 21

Chapter 8: The Sales Professional...………23

Chapter 9: Never, Never, Never Negotiate
Using A Monthly Payment…..27

Chapter 10: Buying From A Private Party.31

Chapter 11: The Power Of Positioning………..35

Chapter 12: The Danger Of Co-signing
             For A Loan…………………………41

Chapter 13: Timing And Power………………..43

Chapter 14: What Am I Buying?………………45

Chapter 15: Learn Everything About
             The Vehicle 49

Chapter 16: Standard Equipment .... .51

Chapter 17: The Test Drive……………………...53

Chapter 18: Back At The Showroom 57

Chapter 19: Take The Next Step………………..61

Chapter 20: What's The Deal With The
             Trade-In? 69

Chapter 21: Finance 73

Chapter 22: Term..77

Chapter 23: Taxes 79

Chapter 24: Extended Warranties....................81

Chapter 25: Leasing Versus Buying..................... 85

Chapter 26: Buying From Rental Companies......89

Chapter 27: Buying Heavy Equipment..............93

Chapter 28: Really Heavy Equipment...............97

Chapter 29: The Keys…………………………...…..103

Chapter 30: Transferable Skills.......................... 107

Chapter 31: From The Author.......................... 119

Chapter 1

Introduction To The Real Deal®
For Smart Car Buyers

I would be willing to bet that you would rather run laps around Texas than visit a showroom of any kind to purchase cars or other vehicles.

It is easy to start thinking that the system is rigged and that somehow, despite your best efforts things don't turn out the way they should when you need to purchase a big ticket, or sometimes even small ticket items. You spent years in high school and college that wasted much of the classroom time avoiding the biggest fact of life. **You will have to negotiate to succeed or be trampled financially every time you buy a car, truck, house, land, or many of the things that make life great.**

For this discussion, automobile purchases make terrific examples of the kind of business that might engage you in negotiations for your money and your future. But the skills in this book will apply to real estate, boats, airplanes, or any negotiable purchase large and small. In reality, all purchases are negotiable because you have the power to just walk away and not spend your dollars at all. It is a form of economic justice that gives you the power to control the marketplace, whether you are the champion of a cause or just keeping your own money.

The best way to get The Real Deal is to understand the styles and backgrounds of sales people. I have been in sales most of my life in order to make a better living than I could make at the average per hour job. Above average salaries, commissions, and bonuses helped me to raise a family as a single mother. I was able to qualify for mortgages on my own and buy property.

In the process, I met and worked alongside sales people who had every selling technique imaginable. No matter what you are buying, the person you are buying from may very well have been consistently in sales, but may have worked in any number of companies, selling any kind of product. Many sales people have in their backgrounds, retail, call center, wholesale products, and services, to name a few. Because of the broad range of experience in different fields, motivation to make a living, and the potential for commissions, you can encounter anything from a fledgling beginner to a real professional who can actually help you get what you want.

Some of the folks I gave copies of the book to, gave me feedback after using the information in the book. They said they were able to use these principles to control what they were spending and used the information during a number of big ticket purchases. So, let's talk about how to get The Real Deal.

When you have been a salesperson your whole life, it can be a strange experience to be the customer. After a washing machine finally stopped working, I went to a local appliance store years ago. I was approached by a nice looking young man in a suit who wanted to know how he could help me. I declared that my last washing machine, from a famous maker, had been the top of the line and lasted for thirty years. I would gladly buy another one and arrange for delivery. What did he reply? "I'll show you our cheapest (yes, he used the word cheapest) model. It is right over here." I was mystified at the response and insulted. Why would anyone assume I was looking for the cheapest thing in the store after I used the words "top of the line"? Did I look like I couldn't afford anything? Should I have worn more expensive jewelry? I left the store and bought what I wanted elsewhere to exercise economic justice. The only way to stop the nonsense is by the use of our dollars. There should be no reward for aggravation. I wondered if the store owner ever knew what happened or whether some sales manager taught this guy to lead people to the cheapest model and then show other models.

Suppose you found that your wallet had been stolen from your pocket, or if you are a woman, someone grabbed your purse and ran with it. Suppose that day you were carrying a couple hundred dollars and now the money was gone along with your credit cards and identification.

You would immediately call the police, start the process of protecting your credit, and lament the loss of the two hundred dollars. Even the wallet or purse might be something special that has serious value.

Yet, every day, people can leave showrooms, closings, and shops paying hundreds or thousands more than other buyers, with all that extra money gone, and no appreciable difference in what they have purchased compared to purchasers who spent less.

Many believe they got a great deal and leave feeling wonderful. To quote a sales manager, "A good deal is a state of mind." They just lost big money by comparison with the stolen wallet and will even pay interest on what they lost, but no one can call the police. No crime has been committed because a contract was signed with the consent of the buyer.

In all fairness, proprietors own the merchandise and have every right to sell products for as much as possible. The same is true in major or minor sales transactions. All skills in the book can be used in any environment.

I have wonderful news! If you read this book from front to back you will probably be so good at getting the best deal that you will have to get your friends to buy copies so that they will stop asking you to go along to help buy a negotiable type of merchandise.

At the very least, pass these tools along to your children so that the next generation will be ready to get The Real Deal. By now you might be wondering who I am and why I want to help you to navigate your way to more money. As a sales person I was a manufacturer's representative, a floral supplier, a new car sales person, an account executive for a waste hauling company, and owned a landscape firm, trying to make a living for myself and my family. I wound up in car sales at one point, because I needed a job and a car simultaneously. I decided that if I sold cars, I would make a living and perhaps pick up a decent one that was being traded in.

Can you imagine being so intimidated about the prospect of buying a car that it was easier to become a car sales person than to go to a showroom as a buyer? I continued over the years to help friends, co-workers, and relatives to buy big ticket items of all sorts. In the process I worked side by side with individual sales people employing all or part of the sales tactics you will read about. The negotiation skills I learned the hard way are totally transferrable to any scenario and any purchase of any kind.

The salesmen who were asked to train me on the product wouldn't cooperate, so I went to the mechanics to see if they would talk to me. They were so happy that a sales person would take the time to know all the things they loved about these vehicles that they armed me with dozens of hidden features to share with customers.

What I am sharing with you took years to find out, buying, selling, and saving a ton of money. I want to give you the power to get a fair deal.

While vehicle purchases are used in the following examples, the same principles apply to negotiation for just about anything. This book was written so that if you encounter any or all of the scenarios I have described, you will be fully prepared to deal with the situation.

You have to read this book from front to back. Do not pick and choose chapters or start in the middle or you will miss important data that will make the difference in the outcome and your ability to be ready for anything that might occur.

❖ All sales experiences are not the same, so I have tried to cover individual elements of negotiation that you might encounter when you are shopping for just about anything.

❖ Using cars in some examples provides an insight into negotiation utilizing a product that most of us will need at some point and the salespeople you will encounter come from every sales background imaginable.

❖ No particular establishment or kind of business has been singled out and salespeople add their own styles learned over the years to the mix, so what you have to be prepared in advance for just about anything. You could encounter any of these sales techniques at any time during the sales presentation for any product.

❖ Businesses try to train their salespeople, but just can't control everything they say and do while they are talking with customers.

❖ We love our cars and new transportation can be important for leisure, travel, and getting to work. It is important for the companies that sell them to make a profit so that there are local places making them available. It is also important to get a deal that is fair to both sides.

Chapter 2

Arriving At The Showroom

Did you know that when you drive in and park your car in front of the showroom you might be under observation even before you get out of the car? The waiting sales people may have already taken recognizance and made judgments about the car you might be trading in, whether it is a two door or four door car (possibly indicating your preferences), the color you chose last time, and whether the car indicates that you are the sporty type or focused on utility.

They might be in the building waiting to see how many people step out of the car and hoping that it will be a husband and wife, because for many salespeople, the belief persists, in spite of all evidence to the contrary, that if a man is involved there will be a better chance that he will qualify for the purchase. The woman might be treated as though she is simply along for the ride, even though her income may be making the purchase possible.

If you are looking for logic, you will not find it in this setting. I am passionate about challenging the way people are treated and together we can give you the power you deserve and that your money commands.

❖   My vision is of an individual walking up the steps to the showroom, bank, or sales office of any kind with an army of more people behind them, backing the buyers, and proclaiming by their numbers that they know what they are doing and commanding respect for their friend. The people peering out the showroom see them and jump back because the rules have changed. We changed them. There is a new force to be reckoned with and respected. Your business and money are running the show.

Chapter 3

The Second You Arrive
Negotiations Have Begun

If you don't remember any other thing in this book remember this. You may have been taught by relatives that negotiation is sitting down at the table and arriving at a price.

Nothing could be further from the truth. Have you ever wondered why it takes so many hours to buy a car? The reason is that there is sufficient time to choose your model, drive the car, find out if you are credit worthy, and gather information that could be influence the price at the time of closing the deal.

When you enter those beautiful doors, you have all the power. Over the next few hours the barrage of data you are given will enhance the product and might convince you on some level that you have less power. So, let's change that!

> ❖ **A huge warning!** During your visit talk only about the car. You will pay more if you divulge family problems, the fact that your car died last week or is on its last legs, any divorce or eminent divorce, any proclivity for rash spending habits, a big ego, competition with your neighbor, becoming a widow, insecurity about your knowledge of cars, or really, just about anything personal. This won't be easy the first time around because you are a regular fair minded person. If

you want the best deal just remember that these folks are not your friends and you will probably never see them again.

❖ Should you bring a friend with you if you don't feel strong enough to say no and you are single? No! Absolutely not! Let me say that again. No! Absolutely not!

Frankly, after my husband saw the truck of his dreams, I went to buy it alone. You see, the problem was that he had been breathing in new truck fragrance. If he had gone to shop with me, this fact could have been detected by the salesmen early on and rendered me ineffective in my mission to get The Real Deal.

Bringing a friend along to protect you could reveal that you appear to be weak prey and exacerbate the idea that you are a person who can't hold his or her own. Your friend will most likely give the salesmen clues and information you might not want them to have. I saw one gentleman railroad his girlfriend into the paying the sticker price of the car with no questions asked.

He knew less about buying a car than most five year olds, but was there as her protector. Vice versa, women can goad men into a bad choice, too. So, don't casually have a friend who has no financial interest in what is being bought to participate. You have no control over what the other person might divulge.

Another helpful gentleman encouraged his female companion to make a really bad decision. This lovely middle aged woman had a low income and a dying vehicle. She brought along her employer. He scorned the idea of buying a used car that I knew was in wonderful condition, priced right, and that she could use for years. The car only had nineteen thousand miles on it, with a potential life of 300,000 miles. She believed that he must know what he was talking about. They left and I never saw her again.

Later the same day, I bought the two year old car that she walked away from, a terrific practical wagon. It handled and sounded exactly like the new ones I was driving every day on test drives. When my customer and her employer drove away, I realized that this little car could save me a ton of money and give me a vast improvement in transportation. At the time, I was driving a high maintenance gas hog. It was so bad that I made jokes that for the money I spent each month in repairs, I could be driving a new luxury car. The previous owner of the car I wanted to buy was a man who believed implicitly that you have to get rid of a car every two years. He provided a public service by trading in perfectly good vehicles and taking the hit on depreciation for the rest of us.

After they left, I went to the management, purchased the car for around $6000.00 and drove it for fifteen years. It survived two sons, who drove it all over town with their band instruments, friends, and various school functions. When the car was seventeen years old, I still used it as leverage to buy a new car. It had no monetary value as a trade, but because it was still looking and working so well, I could honestly say that I really didn't need a car during the final negotiations. If the deal hadn't worked, I still had a car to drive. How could a salesman fight with that? **I had a get-away car.**

One last word about avoiding having a person with you while you are trying to negotiate. There are people in some cities who offer their services to negotiate for you. What do you think is going to happen if they are regular visitors, bringing in clients and selling cars, trucks, or other equipment? Whose side might they really be representing?

Chapter 4

Entering The Showroom

By now you have left your vehicle and someone might even be opening the door for you. After all, you are the customer. Your manner, stature, demeanor, and clothing have all been assessed for an evaluation of your financial status. It pays to look like you have money, because salespeople can make fundamental mistakes about who they are dealing with. They can neglect to show you something at the back of the lot that they know to be a great deal, but pricey. They can even think that you aren't a serious buyer. You'll have to be credit worthy of course, but when you look good you'll find it easier to get waited on. Looking good today might make you feel more confident too.

You might be noticing that the showroom is just magnificent. Remember that later when someone is telling you they sell all their cars below invoice or that they just can't help you with the price you thought you could buy the car for. Where do they find the money for this palace! I think we both know.

> ❖ **Try not to take deep breaths in the showroom at this point. You laugh, but it is loaded with new car smell and all of your senses are brought into play. You see the shiny paint on the perfect cars, the chrome is gleaming, the upholstery is new, and even the tires are spotless.**

Your resolve to do things differently this time is turning to hopeless mush. Before the salesman even speaks, the trap has been set.

"So, were you looking for a particular car today?" he says politely. But he already knows. A person who begins looking for a car will usually purchase one within a few days of the time they step into the first showroom or lot.

Why? Because there is no other reason for anyone to subject themselves to the treatment they have come to expect. In other words, few people would ever go to look at cars just to have fun that day, so if you are there in person, you are in the market.

It doesn't matter when you reply, "We are just looking." and he says "Great!" because he has already fast forwarded to the signing of the documents and a picture of you looking back in your new rear view mirror as you drive away.

Chapter 5

How You Can Get Ready
In Advance

This book is written for women and men, single or married, in any walk of life. If you are a couple, make no assumptions that one of you knows this turf any better than the other. If either party becomes the only decision maker, you might have to be the one who ultimately has to grin and bear it, or get a third job to afford it. Rather than have a situation that calls for compromise at a later date, you need to have a conference prior to driving to the showroom.

Ask yourselves:

❖ What are we looking for?

If You Are Married or a Couple- If your other half wants a sports car, and you feel the need for a wagon, don't go shopping until you agree upon something that meets your mutual needs and budget. You might be the one coping with groceries, the pets, and the children and your needs have to be met to have a smooth running ship. If money is no object, this is less of a burden, but it is still important to know in advance what you both want. Salespeople can exploit the differences between you. You might feel cornered into having a car with a trunk the size of a lunchbox because of the mutual pressure of wanting to make your counterpart happy and the overwhelming sales pressure. Speak up before your influence is diminished.

❖ **If You Are Single- (Couples read this too)** The choice is yours but you need to narrow down to the model you want. Why? You need to avoid being sold a more expensive model than the one you came to see. You see, all businesses have concerns about inventory. For instance, in the car business, it is possible to wind up with too many blue cars, too many four doors, or whatever, in stock. Your needs and wishes are less important than their need to even out inventory or get a particular car off the lot. Once your credit report is accessed with your permission and your ability to buy is analyzed, what you want may be available at your price but you may have to make concessions and get creative. I actually asked a couple who appeared to need a break in the price, "Would you be interested in saving some money on this red car if it was, in reality, blue?" They laughed and we started working on a blue car deal, exactly the same model and features for less money. For some reason, we had just had too many cars of one color. All you had to do was look out the window to see it.

I wrote this book to give you the edge, so I am asking you to resist the impulse to change your plans at the last minute and choose another vehicle. Feel free to smile and politely ask the salesman if he will make up the difference in the price of the car out of his own pocket, if he is suggesting that you buy the next highest priced model, or one with more accessories. That will usually end the discussion.

There is another reason why I strongly suggest that you not shift your focus to another model. You may have studied the prices for the model you came in for. Now, you are considering a different car and you really can't do the math while you are there. All of your research is null and void and you are in a state of confusion. You can only win if you leave in your own car, do the research again, and come back to do this all over again. Who would want to do that? So, know what you came to buy, do the research, and stay with your deal.

❖ **What do we need to know in advance of our trek?**

My friend, you are in the middle of a very serious negotiation. If you don't have an idea of the true value of the vehicle you are considering for purchase, once you are at a showroom, the price is harder to find than the North American Yeti. Even if there is an additional sticker on the car with the suggested retail price, the car may be decked out with accessories that muddy the waters of reason and befuddle the best of us.

You have to have the confidence that comes with knowing that you are absolutely right about the price before you arrive. Do the research on a number of websites. Check more than one. Specific areas of research are listed in another chapter.

Chapter 6

New Car Versus Used

Depending upon the economic environment and other factors there are sometimes good used cars that will take you far on a budget.

If you don't know an engine from a tree, make sure you have an independent mechanic you can trust check the car out and give you an opinion on the car's condition.

❖ **Don't let your mechanic negotiate for you or get involved in buying the car.** Just because he knows the inner workings doesn't mean he ever made a good deal on anything in his life. Pay him for his time looking over the car.

❖ Visit the internet and find the prices that relate to the vehicle and use the same formula for the deal as with new cars. Type in the words "car invoice" into your search bar. Visit multiple websites and try to make sure a particular establishment doesn't own the website.

Chapter 7

What Is The Price?

Years ago salespeople used to walk around with little books containing all the retail and wholesale values. They had access to the information that was limited in the public sector.

Great News! You can go online to websites with all the information you want about the invoice price on the car you want, whether it is new or used. Use the data as a starting point.

You will need to know:

1) **Invoice Price of the new vehicle and suggested retail**

2) **Price of the Accessories available for this vehicle**

3) **Which accessories are Standard Equipment**

4) **Average wholesale price for a car you are trading in**

5) **Retail price of the car you are trading in**

6) **Your own credit report**

21

The price of a vehicle can be driven by market factors like availability, color, and inventory on a particular day. New technologies can temporarily drive up the price of cars or equipment for the opportunity to own the latest upgrades.

However, if you are willing to negotiate, you can buy a vehicle that you can save money on.

Chapter 8

The Sales Professional

It is important to understand the diversity and types of salespeople you might encounter. A real sales professional can be a major asset no matter what you are buying. I would like to give you a few examples to illustrate what I mean.

I considered buying more bricks to enlarge a garden system to grow vegetables in. At a home improvement store, I inquired about the price of delivering a pallet of brick and wanted to know how many bricks are on a pallet (which turned out to be seventy-two). The salesman asked how many I would need and I told him I planned to get one pallet at a time but would need two pallets. He immediately suggested that I should have both delivered at once because the shipping cost of $75.00 would cover both pallets and save me an additional $75.00.

He listened to my initial question, got more information about the number I needed, and made a suggestion based upon knowledge that I would not have known. He made a friend for the store and I will go back there for the product because at another store no one cared.

A sales professional is a person who is driven to know everything about the product he or she is selling and how it will be delivered to the recipient. They know things about how the company is run that will help the consumer. They never stop learning what is new and evaluating how it will appeal to people. In addition, they are confident of their ability to help people make the right decision the first time by finding out what the person is looking for and supplying them with the perfect choice.

Happy customers send in their friends and neighbors and the companies that hire them stay in business.

The last time I purchased a car, the salesman was a disinterested party. He bypassed showing me the car or explaining the features and went on a test drive with me. He did show me the colors available. Since I had to find out more I left. I did the research, decided on the model, and came back the next day.

A sales professional in the car business will know the material in the upholstery and how to clean it. They will know how many cubic feet of trunk space you can expect, all the safety features available, maintenance considerations, and everything about the car. If they don't know, they will take you to the service part of the dealership to get an answer. They never stop learning, and can't stand it if there is something they don't know.

The professional salesman will walk the lot in between customers to find out what cars have come in on trade and their cost. Knowing what else is available is a huge asset in case you are unable to make a deal on a new car, or decided not to spend that much. There are often great alternatives.

A professional salesman is patient, waits for your response, and doesn't try to force you into anything. There are some great salespeople out there and they can make the difference in the value you get for your money.

I personally waited on a couple that came in casually because they were eating lunch across the street. The husband needed a vehicle that could accommodate a wheel chair carrier on the back of the car. I walked the used car lot the night before and knew that we had something they might be interested to know about. The car had unbelievably low miles on it and would work for them, with a huge discounted price. I had inquired about it from the salesman who took it in because I was actually interested in it myself. It had been traded in because the family wanted a different kind of vehicle, like a wagon. They bought the car and I drove it to their home because they had to have the lift for the chair moved from their old car. A fellow salesman drove me back to work. Before they left the showroom, they told my manager that they never intended to buy a car that day and were having lunch across the street, stopping in out of curiosity. They said it was the most expensive hamburger they had ever bought. The wife told the manager that he should give me a raise. He turned to me and said, "OK, here is your raise, go sell another car!"

The point is that a professional salesman will always wait on anyone who comes in, respect their situation, and have enough knowledge to know how to help. Consequently, sales are the natural outcome, so an honest living can be made. The problem is that all salespeople are not professionals.

A while back, my husband and I had figured out exactly what refrigerator we wanted for our new kitchen. At the store, the salesman asked what we were looking for and before we could answer, told us that he had to take a call on his cell phone. He walked off and didn't come back. After ten minutes we walked out of the store in disbelief, went to another store and bought w h a t we needed. A professional salesperson would not have answered the phone, would have taken the money in our outstretched hands and arranged delivery. We were in the middle of the worst recession this area had ever seen and all we read about in the news was that consumer spending was down, that stores were closing, and that people were being laid off. I told my husband that it was no wonder consumers weren't spending any money, because they couldn't get waited on.

Fortunately, there are a lot of excellent sales people out there who take pride in differentiating goods and services for the consumer. They follow up the sale with a phone call to make sure you are happy and ask you to refer any friends that they can assist.

Good sales people cannot be defined by age group, net worth, background, or any normal demographic. They are defined by a constant desire to find out what you are trying to achieve and help you achieve it. They are polite, patient, and interested in solving problems. An excellent salesman will respect the fact that you have gone to the trouble to research your options and have an idea what the price should be. You will be treated with respect.

The important thing is to realize that you will meet all types of salespeople wherever you go and that you are dealing with a diverse group when you are negotiating.

Chapter 9

Never, Never, Never Negotiate Using A MONTHLY PAYMENT!

We need to talk about monthly payments for a moment. You might have noticed that I have focused on the invoice and suggested retail price of the car. If you try to deal backwards from a monthly payment you will lose the deal you want around 90% of the time. I cannot tell you how many people walk in the door and pronounce that they won't make a payment over a certain amount.

The salesman may nod, smile and assure you that he will try to make sure that the payment is within that amount. So many factors are part of the final price that if some additional months are added to the loan contract you get a payment sort of like the one you came for. But if you multiply the months to pay off the loan times the payment you wanted, the price of the car can become astronomical. If this happens, the car is not worth what you are paying for it. Dollars like these could put the kids through college someday or buy better transportation. What is even worse is that the loan can be so high compared to the price of the car that if you try to trade it in at a later date, you could find yourself in a bad situation with the loan amount exceeding the value of the car. Guess what will happen to the difference? If you don't come up with cash to make up the difference, it will be added to the loan on you **next** car, and the cycle of automobile impoverishment continues for another few years. I am counting on you to stop this cycle and start owning your own money.

❖ This is important! Go and buy a little book called an amortization table or get one off the internet. You should at the very least have a calculator or a loan calculator. Take it with you so that you can take a look at what the monthly payment would be if the price of the car is for example, $20,000.00 at an interest rate of 4% for a term of 48 months. You will know the amount of the monthly payment and you will be sure that the payment is correct, relative to the price negotiated, the interest rate and the term.

❖ If you don't know these numbers you have no power and you are toast (meaning you have as much power as a piece of toast). In the shuffle of numbers you could get a fair price on the car and lose some or all your equity in the car you are trading in. If you do well negotiating the price of the car and the trade, you could be offered an interest rate or term of the loan, that will again lose some of what you have gained.

❖ What else should I know in advance?

Get some idea what prevailing interest rates are by going to a bank and checking generally on the rates being offered on car loans. Check your credit union. Check everywhere. If you have a good relationship with your banker, you might be able to get a better rate than the one offered. **Also, don't forget that you can usually refinance a car after you buy it if the rates are more advantageous elsewhere**. If you want to do this, do it as soon as possible, because your new car is already depreciating in value when you drive it off the lot.

People who pay cash for the car don't necessarily get a better deal on vehicles. Surprised? Some companies might do the financing themselves or might make money by arranging loans backed by other companies. If you pay cash, they make less money in the long run, so they will try very hard to get the highest possible price for the car if they aren't involved in procuring your financing. If you are paying cash, never discuss the fact until you have made the deal on the car.

Try to think of negotiating the price as a separate process from negotiating the interest rates. Everything depends on what the prevailing interest rates are at the time you buy. If you are offered a 1% rate on your purchase for the life of the loan, why would you bother with a hefty down payment? On the other hand, if you had a credit problem and were told the interest rate is 12%, you have a major problem that can be solved with a cash down payment to lower the total you have to pay back. You might have to start thinking about a less expensive car or keep what you have for a while. Also, if your credit can be repaired or a mistake is on your report, do what it takes to get it corrected before you arrive to negotiate on a car.

I have to interject a word of caution here. Because of the widespread use of home equity lines, I am hearing people talk about using them for cars because of the lower interest rate. I do not recommend using this source for a vehicle because what you gain in the interest rate, you lose on the term of the loan. You could also jeopardize the ownership of your home if you are unable to pay back the loan. In any case you are decreasing your equity in your most valuable asset.

❖ **Depending upon your age, your retirement could also be affected.** For the sake of your financial well-being, find another way. Sometimes a relative has a car they could sell you or if you are over 65, in some parts of the country, public transportation is a phone call away. Find a way to keep your money. Consider buying from a private party.

❖ What would it cost to take a cab? Could you hire a housekeeper/driver for a few hours through an agency to get you where you need to go for less than car ownership costs?

Chapter 10

Buying From A Private Party

When my youngest son, Scott was nearing the age when he could drive I was able to help him using the principles in this book. To this day, I am very grateful because helping him find his first car was something we could work on together, at a time when teenage sons are rather hard to connect with. Our first jaunt was to the Sheriff's office auction. We looked over what they had that day and decided to bid on a small car that in my opinion should sell for a little over a thousand dollars. Mind you, at this particular auction, we couldn't drive these cars, but there wasn't much risk if the price was low enough. You could listen to the engine and inspect the vehicle, so bidding very much would be a mistake.

The auctioneer was on his way, people got caught up in the competition. We dropped out at our maximum bid and watched when the auctioneer said, "and the winner is…" I whispered to my son, "He is a winner alright! Wait until he finds out he spent $3500.00 on a wholesale car he could get anywhere for around $1200.00 or less! Let's get some lunch!" That day, Scott started walking away from bad deals and not looking back. I was proud of the way he took it in stride.

We then started looking at the cars he found in the newspaper and I taught him to sight down the side of the cars to look for differences in the paint. When you can detect a difference in the paint it can indicate body work on the vehicle. An event or accident may have occurred that could make the car less than desirable. After a while, he could pick out incongruities faster than I could and ask the right questions. I had his respect, which was all I cared about at the time.

Finally, we went to the home of a very nice family selling a car that their daughter would not be taking to a distant college. They told us they were selling it because the insurance was so expensive. We drove the car and it turned out to be solid on the road, but we knew it needed repairs. They were asking $2700.00 and I asked Scott to please let me do the talking and stop looking eager. He really wanted this one.

I asked the husband and wife to realize that Scott had been saving money for a car and didn't have nearly what they hoped to sell the car for. We didn't want to make it difficult for them, but were constrained to a budget of around $700.00 because the car needed a brake service and other work. I explained that Scott would have to handle the insurance bill and do repairs as he made money in order to buy the car. I let them know that overall it was the nicest used car we had seen.

We told them that Scott was willing to transfer the car and pay cash right away so that they could cancel their insurance immediately. We asked them to think about it that night and asked if it would be alright to call the next day. Every step of the way we let them know we would respect whatever decision they made.

The wife walked off with her husband and they talked quietly for a minute. When they came back, they said they would like to go ahead and sell the car to Scott. We thanked them and came back the next day, insured and ready to transfer the title.

When we were on the way home, Scott was very quiet and asked me "How did you do that? They wanted $2700.00 and they could have gotten it." I will never forget the look of admiration on his face. I told him that there was no secret. They wanted out of the car and out of the insurance. It was dead weight and they didn't want to make the repairs and keep the car. But the most important thing was that we had simply explained our position and asked them to consider what we were saying. We made it easy for them to make a decision because we were peaceful and truthful that it was a great little car. It was a sporty car with all the bells and whistles. Scott drove it for years after making about $1200.00 worth of repairs (the number was a constant in our lives for some unknown reason). He worked at a restaurant to pay for everything and bought it before he was old enough to drive. He made his repairs and waited for his sixteenth birthday. Do you think I had to worry that he would be irresponsible with that car? Not for a second.

If you buy a privately owned vehicle, just be straight about what you can do. Realize that people are sometimes emotionally attached to vehicles and want them to go to people they like. Be quiet, peaceful, and thoughtful. If you need a mechanics opinion on the condition, have him come to the home and take a look, but let him know that you want his opinion in private, not in front of the owner because he might inadvertently make a comment that the owner takes to be an insult about his car.

Pay him something for his time, because you might have to repeat the process and his services are not costly compared to making a mistake. You may need him again to check out another car and no one can do this endlessly for free.

You will have to be able to pay a lump sum, because people usually will not carry payments. Make it easy for them and they will make it easy for you. Cash is king in this situation because people generally can't process credit cards and don't want to take a chance on checks.

Chapter 11

The Power Of Positioning

What do I mean by positioning? You will see this in other chapters of The Real Deal book series.

Positioning, for the purpose of getting the best price, is the way and means you have developed for yourself which enable you to get the optimum value for your money. Positioning can help you whether you are wealthy or not wealthy and give you power over what appear to be insurmountable odds.

So, let's talk about positioning as it relates to buying a car.

❖ **Have you checked your credit score?** The folks at the showroom will have to pull (get access to) your credit score and payment habits to even consider selling you a car, truck, or heavy equipment. If your credit score is good and you are known to pay your bills on time, even if you don't make a lot of money, you can still be eligible to buy. The higher the credit score, the better you are positioned to negotiate because they know that you can buy a car anywhere. You can get the deal you want because you are dealing from strength.

❖ **If you have a great credit rating, but don't *know* how good it is, you are not positioned well, and could be led to believe that you don't have any power. So, before you go to shopping, know where you stand.**

❖ **Is your present vehicle still running?** Have you ever known someone who pushed a car so far that by the time they were ready to trade it in, it was dead? Now the trade-in car is gone, a tow truck has to be paid to take the car to the dump, and the car salesman knows that you need a way to get to work. You have not positioned yourself to get the right price because it is hard to radiate confidence when you perceive yourself as defeated. Don't let your car die before you shop for a new one. If it is too late for this advice, come up with a plausible alternative like your Mother is thinking of giving you her car, or something, to get your power back and maximize your positioning.

❖ **Did you arrive at the showroom looking like you are somebody or did you walk in looking like an unmade bed today?** Dress up and position yourself as an independent, smart person, who will not be intimidated. You have to establish that you are a no nonsense person without being aggressive. Remember, we are all behind you! People who look powerful usually are. Your salesman is reading what you look like, so look fantastic.

❖ **Are you determined to use the principles in this book?** If you believe the contents, it could still be hard for you to follow through and actually use the material you have been given. I am asking you to come with me and get what you deserve. If you don't feel powerful yet, just believe that you are, and give it your best. You will be so surprised by the outcome!

❖ **Are you brain washed into believing you have to trade a car in every three years or so?** The biggest proponents of this notion are sales people. They want you to pay top dollar for a new car and take the big hit for depreciation in the first few years. Then they want you to give it back to them soon to sell to another person for a price you probably wouldn't believe, compared to what you will get for the trade.

What a lot of people don't realize is that car technology has made the average vehicle last a very long time with very few problems if the car is properly maintained. Why would you continue a pattern that erodes your wealth? Find out what the average life of your car can be, maintain it according to schedule, and drive it as long as you can. The money you save can be used to invest and grow more money.

A car is not an investment. You may have heard people talk about a car as an investment. An investment is made to make your money make more money. When has a car ever made you money? Even if you write off expenses for a business for income taxes, you don't get to keep the money. You only get to pay less taxes at the end of the year because the deductions reduce your income. That amount could just be a fraction of the cost of the vehicle.

Cars cost you money. They depreciate until they have no value. They rust and turn to dust. Unless you have a fortune and don't care about money (although people who have fortunes **do** care about money most of the time) assess your personal finances and decide what to spend. This is useful information if your salesman suggests that you should invest in a car. You will be positioned to make a good choice. Challenge this and ask with enthusiasm, "So this car is going to give me income? I can't wait to get my first check! When will I get it?"

Don't call me honey! Hold your head high and position yourself to handle deprecating remarks with aplomb. How are you going to negotiate if you allow people to talk down to you? At the first sign of this, speak up politely and assert that you prefer to be called by whatever name you choose. If you feel like you are dealing with piranhas (normally found in the Amazon River), mention that you aren't just buying a car, you are buying a place to go for maintenance. The way you are treated will determine where you spend your money and you are very sensitive about being talked down to. You won't believe how fast piranhas can back paddle.

By the way, I have been asked many times whether women in the car business are more honest than the men. My personal opinion, and you are free to disagree with me, is that it doesn't matter because ultimately your salesperson is only part of the equation. The final decision regarding price will be weighed in by the management, who have to consider all factors.

Positioning has more to do with your true belief system than with the reality of any situation. If you have to practice your lines in the mirror, it will be worth the effort. Think of yourself as a

highly paid actor or actress playing the part of a powerful buyer.

Chapter 12

The Danger Of Co-Signing
For A Loan

Has someone you love asked you to co-sign on a loan? I can't begin to tell you how many times I have heard horror stories from people who decided to help a friend, child, or relative. Perhaps the person's credit was not sufficient to get a loan on a car. So, these nice folks became co-signers on a loan to help them out.

What a lot of them failed to understand was that if the person they were helping ever defaulted on the loan, missed payments, or was routinely late, it would reflect directly on the co-signer's credit report. A person who co-signs on a loan is totally responsible for the loan as much as the person they tried to help out.

People with giving personalities who have been nurturing people all their lives find it almost impossible to say no in a situation like this. If you are one of these folks, I am asking you to take charge and let other people get their own loans without your participation. Your best and perhaps only defense is to stay out of the problem by not physically going to see the car with the person who wants it.

How would you feel if you couldn't buy a car yourself, because someone you co-signed for has ruined your good credit by neglecting to make payments on a loan? Your credit score might not be sufficient to get a car that you need to get to work. It can affect all of your financial dealings if a negative entry shows up on your credit report. The best way to stay out of the co-signer role is just simply avoid going where the car is. Refuse to go there with the person who is asking for your help. It is too easy for nurturing types to get pulled into the wishes of other people and sign on the dotted line as a co-buyer, surrounded by the salesman, the car, and the friend.

Another result of co-signing on a loan could be that if you need additional credit for yourself, you could be denied a higher credit limit on other loans or credit cards. Lending institutions will count the co-signed loan against your income and might perceive you to be over-extended. This can happen even if the person you co-signed for is paying everything right on time and causing no problems.

Heaven forbid that the person you co-signed for allows the car to be repossessed. Do you want to take a chance that your name is attached to that car?

Chapter 13

Timing And Power

Choose a good time of day for yourself, like after breakfast or lunch when you are at your best. Negotiation is going to take you around four to five hours to accomplish, so give yourself time. Choose the portion of the day when you have focus and clarity of mind.

Buying at the end of the month-People have asked me for years whether it is true that it is better to buy a car at the end of the month. My opinion, for whatever it is worth, is yes.

It is no secret that the managers have pressurized goals for the number of cars they need to deliver to customers. In general, each of the cars on the lot is taking up space by the day, which is a business expense. The longer they stay, the more expensive they are to the establishment.

By the end of the month, the push is on to get those cars off the lot and hopefully, parked in **your** garage. Any day is a good day if you know how to negotiate.

If You Can, Buy In December-I bought my last car and my husband's truck at the very end of the year, in December. Why? Again, it is just my opinion, but December, because of the holidays and travel plans is usually not a time when people want to bother with buying cars. Showroom floors tend to look empty, sales are sometimes in the doldrums, and your presence there is coveted. You are in a better position when things are slow. Besides, the establishment is not only dealing with month end figures, but year-end accounting.

If you are a strong negotiator, it will not matter when you make the purchase if you do the research and know where you stand on price.

Chapter 14

What Am I Buying?

Spend a significant amount of time exploring this question. A lot of people think that they are buying a car. Right? Any car or vehicle salesman will tell you that nothing is further from the truth. They know that a lot of people come to buy something like this:

- ❖ A way to get more dates

- ❖ A statement about who you are

- ❖ A way to get noticed

- ❖ A way to impress friends

- ❖ Transportation to and from work

- ❖ A traveling machine

- ❖ A car that will live in two states

- ❖ The penultimate sound system

- ❖ The fountain of youth

- ❖ A home away from home

- ❖ A child-mobile

- ❖ Popularity with the other Mom's

- ❖ A workhorse

- ❖ Recognition of success

- ❖ Acceptance of peers

- ❖ A way to conquer any turf

- ❖ Admiration of friends

- ❖ A way to impress relatives

- ❖ A financial statement

- ❖ A way to feel happy

❖ Showing up an ex-spouse

❖ Protection for your child

These are just a few of the traps you can fall into. You can wind up spending money for something you never intended to buy for a price you could have started an annuity with. **The car you are so attracted to can turn into your really major mistake**. I would like to define what I believe a car really is.

A car is a machine made of multiple hard to reach expensive parts that will convey a person from point A to point B.

I can get anywhere as easily and as fast in my economical car as a billionaire can in a limo. You can only drive the speed limit, so what does it matter if a car can go 200 mph in 60 seconds. Do you really need four wheel drive in Miami, where the highest altitude you can drive to is in a parking garage? Will you really get more dates in a convertible?

Is your future father in law going to change his opinions at all because you own this car? Does having this car really prove that you are rich?

Chapter 15

Learn Everything About The Vehicle

If your salesman sort of waves at the car and wants to know what you want to do, get another salesman. A good salesman should lift the hood and take you through the engine, to the interior of the car and on to the inside of the storage sections so that you will know what you are buying. Clarify the safety features, upholstery, etc. You should have a chance to ask questions about the car, the existing warranty, any promotions that are running, and the availability of the color you want.

Don't let anyone rush you. You have set aside time, driven to the showroom, and they are going to keep you busy for the next few hours anyway. Remember, you have already started the negotiation process and you have to maintain control of the situation to get the deal you came for.

In the showroom, sit down in the front seat for a few minutes and get the feel of the contours and the seat levels to see if the car is going to be comfortable over a long period of time. There is nothing worse than finding out on a long trip that your back is aching, you feel like you are pushing the whole car down the road with your right foot, or that you have a headache from the glare off of a giant dashboard.

Ask about the frequency of maintenance, the cost of maintenance, and the expected mileage. A gas hog can break your bank down the road. What kind of tires come with the car? How many miles can you expect out of them before you have to buy new ones?

Can you see out well or do you feel like the visibility is inhibited in some way. Maybe for a taller person this would be a great car, but for you, it feels like you are inside an army tank.

> ❖ **Review what the car comes with, versus added on accessories. The Real Deal question to ask is:**

What is standard equipment?

Chapter 16

Standard Equipment

As we discussed, the price of the car can be a moving target if you don't know what the car comes with at the invoice price.

You see, the invoice price you found on the internet at a car invoice comparison site includes all the accessories that come as standard equipment. If the car has something like a DVD player that is not standard equipment, and it is already installed in the car, a value might be assigned to it that is much higher than you would expect to find in a retail store. A $40.00 radio is suddenly listed at some enormous price. So, if you aren't ready for this, you could pay vastly more than the ordinary price for an accessory (just because it is already installed in the car you are buying!) and then **pay interest** on it for the next few years too.

There is a powerful alternative. **Buy the vehicle with only the standard equipment. If they tell you an expensive accessory is already on the car, tell them to remove it or order a new car that has nothing but the standard equipment. There is no comparison between a few days wait compared to years of higher payments.** If they won't comply, let them know you are leaving. Politely thank them for their time, and physically head for your vehicle. You might be surprised to find that they won't let you leave after all, and that there is room for compromise.

You have options if you find a great car and need to pay less. You can let the salesman know you will be willing to wait for a car to arrive from the manufacturer without the add-ons and for him to call you when it arrives, remove the add-on on a car presently on the lot, or lower the price of the add-on as part of the deal.

Why pay interest for years on a special radio? You can buy it for cash at a radio shop and have it installed later. It doesn't become part of a car loan. Keep your money in your pocket and get the same product and satisfaction.

Chapter 17

The Test Drive

So far, you've done a great job and followed the instructions in the book. I want you to get behind the wheel and see how the car handles and whether it is really what you want. If you buy a car without driving it, you could be making a huge mistake that you will regret every time you have to go anywhere.

It is not a bad idea to test drive the car a day ahead of making the deal on it. You need to be sure of your selection and complete your research on the car.

Your salesman will probably drive you out of the car lot and navigate you to a quiet neighborhood where he won't be in much peril with you behind the wheel. He will most likely try to put you in an upscale environment where everything is neat and lovely, because you will be glad that you are in this location in your new car, instead of your old one. Your salesman wants you to take possession of this vehicle and consider it your own. He wants you to bond with the car.

> ❖ **Did you know that your salesman might wait to ask some key questions for the moment you are behind the wheel? This is just a personal observation, but I have noticed over the years that it is very difficult to deflect a direct question when you are driving.**

I believe the reason is that you are concentrating on the road and questions become a secondary thing for you to handle. Because of this you will tend to answer a direct question with the first thing you come up with, the whole truth, in an instant. This can work against you in later negotiations.

❖ **Just a note:** I once used this principle to find out the identity of a person that a business partner had hired. Every time I asked about a new recruit I got an evasive answer regarding why he was among us. We were struggling with payroll at the time and I wanted answers.

I waited until he was driving and asked him directly why this new person was in our midst and if he was somehow related to him. He answered that the young man was his ex-girlfriend's son, that he owed her money and that by giving her son a job, he was paying her off. Then he looked at me like he couldn't believe he had just blurted out the truth.

The recruit and the partnership were quickly terminated.

Suppose you are a single woman on the test drive. Your salesman might ask you if you like the way the car handles. You might reply that it is certainly better than the car you own. So, he knows that this is definitely a plus. No harm is done to your negotiation positioning because you haven't revealed much personal data.

Now suppose that out of the blue, he asks if this car will make your trip to work more pleasant. You are concentrating on the road and you might shoot back "It really would because I am a field representative and spend a lot of time in my car going to see customers." "No kidding", he says, "What company are you with?" You reply that you are with a large national retailer.

He now has a tremendous edge during negotiations because he knows you are the only buyer that he has to deal with, you are ready for more comfort, and perhaps more prestige. You have a sales presence and your customers might see you in your car. You probably make above average income. He also knows that you have a busy schedule, your time is limited and you probably want to just get it over with. Therefore, the salesman has information that will make it possible to aggressively attempt to get more money for the car and complete the deal today.

To get the deal you came for:

1. Keep the test drive a reasonable length of around 25-30 minutes.

2. Before you answer anything, pause for a moment, think it through, and carefully phrase a response.

3. Avoid answering a lot of questions.

4. Ask your salesman about the car or maintenance.

Chapter 18

Back At The Showroom

You have arrived back at the showroom and parked the car. It is possible that your salesman will offer to check the inventory to see if the car is available.

You might shriek, "What do you mean? I told you this is the car I am interested in!" So, he now knows that you are interested in this particular car and will ask you to come inside to his office, while he checks inventory. He might come back with the wonderful news that the car is available, but they only have one. An element of urgency has manifested itself. I actually came back from a test drive to find out the car we had just driven was sold to another customer while we were out on the road.

I Have Great News! There are more being manufactured every day! You Can Still Get One!

❖ You might be in a cubicle on the sales floor or in a glassed in office. Surveillance is so common in retail stores and parking lots that we have all come to expect it. In fact many of us are very glad it is present for security reasons. Most businesses also have surveillance in place to keep track of what is transpiring during the day. In most businesses, managers keep a close eye on their sales people to see how they are progressing and what they are doing. We are all accustomed to this sort of thing whether we are in a clothing store or a shopping mall environment. The difference here is that you are not spending a few dollars of expendable income. You are spending thousands of dollars.

What you have to remember is that your body language and speech patterns can give away signals that you are losing your resolve to see your deal through to your satisfaction. If you say you are sure what you are paying for this car and your body language shows that you aren't relaxed and sure of yourself, you are on the way to losing your negotiating position.

Stay relaxed and comfortable. Remember that this is your money and that you don't have to do anything at all today or any day. If an agreement can be reached that is wonderful, but if it can't you will go somewhere else. You have the final say not the seller.

You are finally ready to discuss the price of the car. The salesman begins pecking away at a calculator like a statistician, adds up the damages, and shows you the total cost of the car. Like the price is an absolute. He might ask, casually, if you are trading in your vehicle.

❖ **Keep the trade out of the deal or you can become lost on the cost of the new car.** At this point, tell him you haven't decided what you are doing with your car and that you only want to concentrate on the price of the car you are buying.

You are getting sleepy, laced with discomfort. After all, you have just read a book about this, but what if you can't pull it off. What if they laugh at you? What if they ask you to leave?

Relax. They want to sell a car. They don't want you to leave. Pretend that you have a hide like an alligator. This is your money and your life. You have the power. Repeat to yourself, "It is my money and I have all the power regarding this decision."

Chapter 19

Take The Next Step

It is your turn to present what you think is a fair deal. Tell your salesman about your research. You know the invoice price of the car and are willing to pay whatever you feel is fair. In addition, you will not pay inflated prices for any accessories that come with the car as non-standard equipment. You understand that manufacturers sometimes offer their best prices to huge retailers and that you believe that your calculation is fair to both sides. Remember those commercials you've seen about buying at invoice? If you neglect the research you won't know what invoice is.

High volume stores might possibly pay less than invoice prices you saw on the internet for the car because manufacturers have the option to give rewards for the volume at a particular car lot. But at the same time, your research will be the best barometer for your offer.

It is imperative that you know your numbers before you even drive the car. If you are completely off base with a request that has no basis in reality, like some price so low that you couldn't buy a bicycle with it, you will be considered misinformed and not a serious customer. In cases like this, you will be politely dismissed in a kind way, as someone not worthy of spending time on.

I once had a customer who declared right away that she wouldn't pay over $7000.00 for a new car that priced out at $20,000.00 at the time. Apparently, she actually believed at some level that this was possible or had inaccurate information that she was depending upon. Ultimately she left without a new car because what she wanted could not be done. So, you have to be fair in the sense that you are aware that the seller has to make a profit to stay in business. On the other hand, you don't want to find out too late that you have paid thousands more than some neighbor down the street. You have to be prepared to seek fairness and base your opinions upon sound research.

- ❖ Be Polite

- ❖ Be Prepared

- ❖ Be Firm

- ❖ Be Fair to Yourself

- ❖ Do not be Confrontational

- ❖ Don't show Anger

- ❖ Deal from Strength

At this point, the person across the table from you should be looking a little dazed (but some have a hide like an alligator too and might smirk). Because you have been so business minded and polite, he might not know what to

do with you, except to tell you that no car has ever been sold for that price.

Start Thinking That You Are Listening to a Quacking Duck And Pay No Attention to the Words.

❖ One thing that I would like to stress to everyone is that it is easy to become outraged at the manner, tone, and posturing of salesmen. I have been on the wrong end of a sneer more than once myself. You may have become super sensitive to this kind of behavior in the past. You may have a razor tongue and a sharp wit and want to use it on them.

If you want to win, you have to put all that away and become the soul of serenity and kindness. If you become aggressive in speech or tone, they will win and have you apologizing too. In the end, it's about the money and I want you to keep as much of your money as possible.

❖ **Repeat your points every time someone tries to convince you that you don't know what you are talking about:**

I have good credit.
I have done heavy research.
I know the numbers.

My facts are correct.
I can buy this car anywhere.

It is now time to take a deep breath of new car fragrance and go into the battle for your own money. Smile and mention that you had really hoped to be able to do business with this particular establishment because they were highly recommended and they are close to your house, or something that sounds reasonable. You can understand that they might not do as much volume as some of the competitors in the area. Then, don't say anything else and don't get up out of your chair.

 ❖ Your salesman now has to go to the sales manager and present what is happening in his cubicle. He may reach for the phone and it may seem like he is talking to the head of a major car company in a foreign country to discuss what you want. The manager is rarely more than thirty feet away and will usually call the salesman in for a conference to find out the details that have accumulated about your transaction. The prior hours of conversation will be revisited to find any compelling reason why you might not be so strong in your convictions.

 Finally, the salesman might come back and suggest that they have done everything they can, but this is a very popular model, they don't have many of these, and the manager said they just can't take more than $500.00 off the price of the car.

 ❖ **Please note that you were just told a short time before that the price was an absolute. It can**

happen that if you have done a good job of scoping out a fair price for the vehicle, the salesman might come back with the news that you can purchase the car for the price you expect. You may have the numbers dead right and they are willing to sell the car without any further negotiation. But if you are sure your numbers are right and can't get an agreement, you will have to continue negotiating.

Begin repeating your message. Calmly address the gentleman before you as if you are nobility, and thank him for his time today. You have been very impressed with the car and truly want to buy it, but have decided what you will pay, based upon your research. The price you will pay is a total of Blah, Blah, Blah, and you want to be fair, but simply will not put that much money into the car.

Be wonderfully polite and slow things down if you feel rushed. Keep looking in your amortization book and going over the numbers. Substantiate your research with real data.

Keep mentioning that you can't work with the numbers they are presenting and will have to come back another day or go elsewhere to buy a car (by the way, take a second to look up the name of the nearest competitor, and make sure they don't own another lot nearby).

Consider other Models or Makes: Let them know that while you like this car, you also have developed a fondness for a car of an entirely different brand and perhaps should look at that one too.

You are creating the beginning of an exit. Only so many customers will arrive today. It is very important to get as many cars delivered as possible. Precious time has been spent with you and it is important that you buy the car here or all the time spent with you is wasted.

Car lots are strange places and the people who run them might seem to have bad cases of short term memory. If a sales manager has had a bad week or day, you will get what you want in less time, maybe four hours. Sometimes, if they have had a couple of outstanding weeks, they get cocky and will allow a real customer to leave thinking the deal can't be done, only to call a couple of days later at home with the deal they could have done at any time. Hopefully, if this happens to you, you can let them know you already bought the car elsewhere. The only thing for sure is that you have to stick to your research and ride out the negotiations until you get what you want. You will not get what you want unless you are actually willing to walk away from the deal entirely.

Tactics that could be used to get your dollars:

❖ **Intimidation**
❖ **Humor**
❖ **Sympathy**
❖ **Camaraderie**

At some point, the sales manager or another salesman might join you to sit down and talk things over. This person will try to alleviate the impasse or whatever obstacle seems to be holding up delivery of the car. The belief at some places, is that if you are offered a new face to deal with, you might be more apt to work with the new person or find a way to solve a problem you have not mentioned yet.

Why? Because it is recognized that you might just have a personality conflict or not like your salesman. To keep from losing any precious customer, you might be given the opportunity to speak with someone else before you leave without a new car.

With your permission, they have checked your credit and know whether you are someone who can qualify to buy a car. If you are a qualified customer, they want you to leave in their car. If a salesman or manager joins the conversation he will usually go over the numbers and suggest a compromise. Alternatively, he might take a hard stance that your price cannot be met.

A Note- Why not ask for the sales manager when you arrive? Because sales managers are incredibly busy working on car deals, have very little time, and depend upon their sales people to take care of customers. They are wasting time talking with anyone who has not been deemed credit worthy, landed a particular car, driven the car and expressed a genuine desire to buy. In my opinion that is a fair stance. Do not waste your time asking for the sales manager when you first walk in the door. If you do you will look inexperienced, hurt your position, and end up with your sales person anyway.

Don't bring your trade into the deal until you have established the price you are paying for the new or used vehicle you want to purchase.

If your offer is not accepted and you know from your research that it is reasonable, stand up to go. That is the only way that they can recognize you are serious, that you will actually terminate the discussion if you don't get what you want. You have to be prepared to walk away from the deal and show that you are not a weak person.

When you are at the number you offered or very close to the number your research has led you to, you can shake hands on that part and thank them for working with you.

When you love the car, the color, and want new transportation it is much easier to give in and take the deal offered than it is to turn it down. Car shopping is wearing and going through the process again and again is beyond fatiguing. Try to think of how you will feel if you don't get the deal you need and you have to look at a ridiculous bill every month for years.

❖ **Now, and only now, bring in the subject of the trade.**

Chapter 20

What's The Deal With
The Trade-In?

The car you are trading in is actually a more complex issue to deal with than the one you are buying. Unlike a new car, it has a history and how it has been maintained, whether it has been in an accident, body work, interior condition, and all sorts of issues can contribute to exactly what it is worth.

However, if you can stand back and be objective, you will get some very good guidelines regarding the wholesale value of your car from the internet. If you can sell the car for cash you might get a better price dealing with the general public. This is always an option.

Why don't more people put an ad in the paper and sell their own cars? Because it is easier to get rid of the old one at the same time you buy the new one.

Private sellers have an extra problem and the people in the business are aware of it. If you advertise your car and someone you don't know comes to your door to test drive the car, you could be in a dangerous position. What if this person is a car thief or worse, passes bad checks on a daily basis, or just wants to case your house for a future robbery? Unless you are selling the car to someone you know, like a neighbor, it might be a good idea to use the principles in this book to get what you want in a safe environment.

Knowing the approximate value of the trade-in car will help you to determine if you are being treated fairly and whether to trade the car in or sell it privately. Appraisers will only pay the wholesale value of the car, because they have to do repairs and sell it in a short time. They also might have to pay for damage to be repaired to the body or for new parts. You have to be objective about your good old car and assess the value according to the real condition of the car.

Take some time to clean and wax your vehicle before trading it in. The small amount of time you spend could get you more money. If you drive in a car with banana peelings on the floor you are exhibiting that you don't value the car, so why should the appraiser think differently.

After a certain number of years, your car has no resale value at all. A car with no book value is sometimes referred as a wholesale piece in the business, and is usually sold for a very tiny price to one of the buy here pay here lots down the street. But such a car can still serve you well as a get-away car, in the event you need to let people know that you still have transportation and don't need their car at all.

❖ What to do if you are upside down-

If you owe more money on your car than what the car is worth, any banker will tell you that you are upside down. What they mean is that in order to pay off the loan on your car you will have to pay the difference between what they are paying you for the trade-in car and the loan that you still owe on it. You will find yourself in an adverse position. The money to make up the difference will have to come from you. If you decide to move ahead with this deal, you will have to come up with the cash to cover the difference. If you don't have the cash, the difference will be tacked on to the price of the new car, causing you to have a higher loan for the new car. I would advise you to back away from doing this because it leads to years of continued overpayment for your transportation.

If you can, try to pay off the car you are in to lower the final price. At the very least, don't owe more on the car you are trading in than what you can get paid for it.

Chapter 21

Finance

You could be in your fourth hour at the place and think you are finished with negotiating. I congratulate you for reading this book and working to get the best deal possible. I know you have done a great job so far!

You are tired and happy because you have the car you want at the price you want. **Right?**

Not necessarily. You might be introduced to another office and another gentleman or woman, your finance and warranty person. In general, you couldn't meet a more personable person. These folks are chosen for their passion for the numbers and stage presence.

They meet all the customers, so their time is limited. To speed things up, they talk a little faster and sometimes will tap a pencil or pen while you are trying to think. You might take the message to mean "hurry up, hurry up, hurry up, we don't have time for thinking around here".

This is a great time to slow things down. Was anyone in a hurry to do anything during the last few hours? Why should you feel any need to progress at any other than your own pace?

Finance and warranty departments are in many ways as much or more of a money making arm of the establishment as the car sales department, and I urge you to respect their power and have more power.

Why are there people in place to offer on the spot loans, extended warranties, etc.? Because they might make money on your loan, and extended warranties or the convenience of this service makes it possible to move a car, enhancing volume and profit.

The good thing is that if you can qualify in any way for a car, even if you have difficult credit or other issues, they might have a lender behind them who will get you a loan, quicker and easier than your average dear banker. But let's assume for a moment that you have pretty good credit score, which you know because you checked before you left home.

If you are uncomfortable about the interest rate, term of a loan, products, or anything about the offering, stop all the action on the car and let them know that you will not take this car today unless your concerns are addressed. You may have to be very firm in your resolve to convince them that you mean it.

❖ **You have to be able to leave without the car today or you have no power.**

Ask about the best interest rate that can be offered. Let them know you have other sources of financing. You can leave in your own car and shop for a better interest rate at a bank. This gives you an additional control factor, because they haven't sold your car while you are looking around.

Alternatively, you can request the right to shop for a few days for a better rate elsewhere, while driving the new car.

Just make sure your right to replace their loan with a new one within a specified number of days is noted on the contract for purchase in writing and that no penalties will be paid if you find financing elsewhere. Ask the finance person to sign or initial that phrase.

One drawback you have is that if you are not able to get a better rate, they will have sold your trade-in car as soon as they possibly can, so you are stuck with the deal you have. I only suggest this method if you know your credit is so strong that you can get a better deal. Don't be shy about anything that you want to explore.

I will share a story about the car I am still driving. The last time I purchased a car, I was presented with an interest rate that I considered too high. I thanked them for their time and rose to leave (I had worked with them for four hours by then). They called the salesman who came charging up to take me to my car in a golf cart. My good old car was only a hundred feet away (such drama!).

On the way, he got on the phone with the manager again and they offered to give me more money for my trade-in to help defray the cost of the higher interest rate. Now the joke is that the car I was trading in had absolutely no value, it was seventeen years old! I told him that I would take the deal he was offering me on one condition, that I would be allowed to obtain a better interest rate and replace the loan within five days with no penalty. I completed the deal and drove my new car to two banks.

I filled out two loan applications, which triggered inquiries from the banks on my credit report. I speculated that the salesmen would pull my credit report to see if I was actually out there trying to get better financing. A couple of days later, before the banks even responded, I got a call that went like this:

"Mrs. Balk, the most wonderful thing has happened. We have a new vendor who is able to reduce the interest rate we quoted you by four percent. All you have to do is come in and re-sign the paperwork." I went in and carefully reviewed the paperwork to be sure that no other changes had been made, signed the paperwork, and came out of the place four percent richer on the loan. I still got to keep the extra money they gave me to defray the expense of the interest too. I paid off the car early and saved even more. The car came with a ten year standard warranty, tires for life, and a five year road service at no extra cost. One of the bankers I went to told me that she had never seen anyone come in with a price so low on that car. They beat the rates the banks offered me, and knew what they had to beat.

❖ Remember that the finance officer has numerous lenders at his disposal and depending upon the relationships with those vendors may be trying to get more volume with a particular institution. Your welfare might not be the guiding star in his choice of lenders and corresponding interest rates. You have to be ready to take care of yourself in this department.

Chapter 22

Term

If you get everything else right and get the term of the loan on your new car wrong, you can lose almost all of your gains. Let's look at three total payments created by the term of the loan with all other factors being equal.

1. $20,000.00 X   3 yrs (36 Months) @ 6% = 608.44/mo

2. $20,000.00 X   4 yrs (48 Months) @ 6% = 469.70/mo

3. $20,000.00 X   5 yrs (60 Months) @ 6% = 386.66/mo

Effect on the total price:

1. 36 months X 608.44 = 21,903.84   Total Price Paid

   Total Interest Paid = 1,903.84

2. 48 Months X 469.70 = 22,545.60   Total Price Paid

   Total Interest Paid = 2545.60

3. 60 Months X 386.66 = 23,199.60   Total Price Paid

   Total Interest Paid = 3199.60

In this example, the person who took financing for 60 months added a total of 3,199.60 to the original price of the car.

This is why that wonderful little amortization table book can be a priceless resource. You will know what you are paying and take control of how you want to spend your money.

So, if you pay cash you don't pay any interest, right?

This is correct, but be aware that you are going to really have to know the right price for the car and do your research. If interest rates are very low and not variable, you might be better off to take a loan and let your cash work for you. Only you can make this decision.

If you are going to pay cash, I suggest not mentioning it until you have negotiated the price of the car, including the trade-in values.

Chapter 23

Taxes

The total taxes added to your car contract will be based upon the price you negotiate, making that price all the more important. The less you pay for the car, the less you pay in taxes. Your tax bill will also depend upon where you live and current legislation.

Do you really want to pay **interest** on *taxes* for the term of your loan? Even if you get a loan with the lowest interest rate possible in the world, I would urge you to at least make a down payment that will pay for all of the taxes on the car.

Chapter 24

Extended Warranties

By now, you are being asked to think about extended warranties. These warranties are often additional warranties to the standard warranty that comes with the car. Ask your finance person if there is any **overlap** on the policies.

As an example, a car might have a three year warranty from the manufacturer at no extra cost. If you purchased an extra warranty for three years, depending on the product, you need to know if it starts at the end of the other warranty or whether it will overlap an existing standard warranty. Read the policy carefully to confirm whether it overlaps a year that is already covered or if there are enhancements not covered by the standard warranty. Make a decision based upon the facts.

Ask about exclusions in the policy and read them. You might find the exclusions and limitations to coverage so dense that it would be harder to get the warranty company to pay off on much of anything than it would be to ride a roller coaster standing on your head with no handlebars. On the other hand, the policy could be something with real merit. In the end, only you can decide this and if there is ever a need for the extra warranty you might be glad you have it. Just find a way to read what you are buying.

Your finance person is probably very busy tapping that pen right now and will want you out of the office, so ask if you have to take the warranty now or whether you can read it at home so you'll know what you are buying. Ask how long you have to cancel the warranty or other add-on products after buying the car, if you change your mind. Based upon the answers, try to make the best decision you can. Then, close the deal on the car if everything is the way you want it. If you are confused, uncomfortable or being rushed, leave without the car.

Any cost that you include as part of a loan might affect interest paid over the term of the loan. **Make sure what the rules are for canceling the warranty and how many days you have to exercise your rights without any penalties if you buy it as part of the car purchase or by itself.**

The laws for grace periods or cancellation of purchase contracts vary from state to state. Make sure you understand the laws in your state and what you are committing to.

Protect Yourself With Insurance:

The warranties and add-on products sold in a car transaction are generally not the type of auto insurance sold by your local property and casualty insurance agent to satisfy the laws in your state.

The rules differ from state to state. It is my opinion that you should not drive your new car without calling your insurance agent, letting them know that you have a new car, and adding it to your policy, even if you have the right to more time by law. You might forget to call later. If you get into an accident and you are not covered, the consequences could be enormous. Rules differ according to state laws, so know the rules. It is just easier to call your agent before you drive, without delay, and take care of this so you won't forget.

If this is your first car, shop for insurance before you get the car and call your agent before you drive it. Shopping for insurance in advance can sometimes help you decide which car to buy. Some cars are so expensive to insure that your car payment will be the least of your worries.

I once showed a young man a used sports car. He wanted the car very badly, but I suggested that he check on the price of insurance at his age, for that particular car. I also asked him to call a mechanic and find out about the cost of regular maintenance on the vehicle. He left and called me later that day with the news that he learned about the precision tune-up and ongoing costs. Needless to say, he started looking at different models.

If you haven't bought insurance, leave the car at the car lot if you have to, until you talk with an insurance agent and arrange coverage according to their instructions. They will have to set up coverage and inspect your new vehicle. Get the insurance agent's advice on how to handle the situation in your state. Do not procrastinate and don't drive a vehicle unless you are properly insured. You might have to leave the car parked and not drive it until you make insurance arrangements.

Anything can happen at any time when you are driving. The consequences of not having appropriate insurance can follow you for years, cost you a fortune, ruin your credit, and wreck your finances if you get into an accident that creates a financial liability.

Underwriters of insurance take a dim view of what they consider total irresponsibility because as they see it, by driving without insurance, you are not only disregarding your own wellbeing, but the safety and care of others.

You could wind up with a destroyed car and still have to pay off the car loan. In addition, the policy that you will buy next will be astronomical beyond your capacity to believe the bill when you see it. Believe me, you don't want to pay the kinds of premiums created when the insurers find out a person had no insurance at the time of an accident.

Chapter 25

Leasing Versus Buying

You may be offered the opportunity to lease instead of buying a car. You have to know what leasing is and how it can affect your bottom line.

When you lease a car, you choose a term during which you pay for an agreed upon price. Theoretically, the price should be less than it would be if you purchased the car. A residual amount should be subtracted from the price of the car, because you are only using up part of the life of the car, and the folks you buy it from will sell it at the end of the lease. The residual amount (expressed as a percentage) varies with make and model. Find out the residual percentage for that particular car. Residual percentages can be vastly different from car to car. Subtract it from the total price you have researched for the car. Divide the remainder by the number of months you are leasing and that should be your lease payment before interest. Find out how much interest or other money is being tacked on and why. Don't let anyone rush you in understanding the figures. Having a pocket calculator or loan calculator can be useful because unless you are a genius, you will not be able to figure out the right price.

Since you don't own the car and will be bringing it back at the end of the term, the owner has the option of selling their car after the period of the lease ends. Look for conditions on leased cars, like the amount of insurance you have to carry, the type of insurance you have to carry, (because they own the car, not you), and most significantly, the number of miles you can drive the car without an extra charge. If you exceed the mileage agreed upon in the contract, you might have to pay a significant per mile charge. If you leased to save money, and exceed the agreed upon mileage, you will ruin your budget. For instance, if you get a new job with a long commute the lease might wind up costing more than you had counted on.

Sometimes, if it is part of the contract, you can purchase the car at the end of the lease, but make sure that you have the entire deal hammered out in the beginning. Lease prices are negotiable just like any other prices, so know the residual value (value left after the lease period), and all the other steps in this book.

Even though you don't own the car, you generally have to insure the car at a level agreed upon in the contract. They will require you to buy it to protect their car, because it is an asset that can be destroyed.

Lastly, the day will come when you have to bring in the car and once again decide whether you want to buy a car or lease another car. When you buy a car, you have the option of trading it in whenever you are ready. When you lease a car, you have to turn the car back in on a certain date.

When you return the car, depending upon your contract, the car might be inspected and if deficiencies are found, you also might be penalized monetarily for those deficiencies depending upon your contract. Read the entire contract before making a decision to lease to make sure the provisions are consumer friendly and meet your needs.

So, when does a lease make sense? It would make sense, for example, for a person who buys a new car frequently, who can stay within the mileage range, and has an income that can be predicted to continue reliably for several years ahead.

Before you sign any contract, make sure the numbers reflect everything you have talked about in the last few hours. Make sure everything is correct and don't sign anything if you still have questions.

Chapter 26

Buying From Rental Companies

Purchasing a vehicle from a rental company can be another way to save money, if you use the same negotiation tactics that are in this book. It is no different than the usual negotiation experience except in a couple of very important ways.

The car may have been driven hard by travelers who rented it or dented it. You have to look hard at the car, the interior, lights, cleanliness, windows sliding easily, air conditioning, and drive the car to get a sense of the condition.

The car has already depreciated and is worth less than its new counterpart, based upon the mileage and time the car has been on the road. It wouldn't be a bad idea to have a device with internet access to be able to get instant estimates of the invoice value of that particular depreciated car.

If you really want to know if a car you want has defects, rent it and drive it for a couple of days. You have no stake in the car. When we rent a v e h i c l e we always buy the insurance offered by the rental company. Surprised?

I have had a difference of opinion over the years with people who think it is a waste of money to buy insurance from the rental company when renting a car. My stance is that if you get into an accident, instead of turning in the car and leaving the problem behind, your personal insurance might have to pay for damages. If so, you might have the wonderful opportunity to watch your insurance policy go up in price for the next few years depending on state statutes. It could be the most expensive vacation a person could ever take.

One evening on a family vacation, with elderly family members in the car, someone tossed raw eggs off a tall building in San Francisco on the cars below. It probably sounds ridiculous, but you can't imagine the startling impact an egg can make on the roof of the car and the eggs went all over the windows, limiting vision. We got the windows cleared right away to drive. The next morning, in the light, we realized that there were dents in the roof like hail and that the eggshell had made lines in the paint.

It was great to be able to drive the car in, tell them what had happened and turn in the keys with no questions asked and no liability. I will always buy the insurance.

My husband and I had a landscaping business years ago. We actually rented a 350 dual wheeled truck for a landscaping job and it worked out so well for the crew members that I looked into buying it from the rental place as the official family car buyer. By the time we turned it in after renting it, we were learned that they had already rented out the truck to a couple who wanted to see the fall leaves up north. The truck was gone for weeks and there wasn't another one they would sell at the time. The folks put a few thousand miles on the truck before arriving back in town.

We had the time to hunt locally for the truck and got some really bad news. They were going for outrageous prices because of the proximity of gorgeous horse farms and polo.

Price was no object for these folks and the trucks were decked out for tailgate parties on the weekends. Dual wheeled 350's were almost unaffordable to people in the small trades. We went to the rental place and rented it again to make sure everything was good after its long trek and because of the advanced mileage were able to buy it for almost 30% less than the going rate. We sold it 10 years later to another tradesman who was happy to get it now that prices were even higher than before. So, rental cars and trucks can be a really good deal if you know the market and if you can drive for a day or so to make sure of the handling. Definitely look it over before buying. You still have to negotiate the price and use all the considerations in the book to get The Real Deal.

Chapter 27

Buying Heavy Equipment

Buying equipment like tractors and big landscaping equipment can be an experience that makes car shopping look very tame. It can be very difficult to even choose which manufacturer has the right set of features for your needs until you physically take one out on a job and put it through its paces. The cost of heavy equipment can make or break a business to the point where some contractors always rent and never own any equipment outright. Some win and some lose in the game of building. If your business is very successful and you buy equipment, you can definitely come out ahead because you are always ready at a moment's notice to tackle a job. If you have a good operator, it can be money in the bank. But let's say there is a real estate downturn and you are in debt for the big machines. You can wind up losing the machine and money in the business simultaneously. As a contractor you might never recover.

It is so important to choose the best equipment for the work. I suggest that before you buy, even though it costs more money incrementally, that you rent different trucks and machines to see how they suit the work you are trying to accomplish. It is better to spend some money on rental than to get trapped into the wrong equipment.

Once you decide what model you like, it is time to go shopping. The heavy equipment purchasing experience can eclipse anything you would ever imagine compared to buying a regular vehicle. When we bought landscaping equipment it was definitely a challenge every time.

We needed a heavy duty diesel engine, to pull equipment trailers for a landscaping business. In addition, a strong articulating loader was essential for moving trees and plants. If you have good credit and experience in your trade, buying equipment wouldn't seem to be much of a challenge. We began renting trucks at a local rental place because there were contracts to fulfill. One truck was perfect for our needs and I inquired about the price. I was able to buy the truck from the rental place, as I mentioned previously in the book. It only had a few thousand miles on it from rentals and they had made a lot of money renting it, so the price was drastically reduced on an almost new truck. The truck had ample room for all of us, a huge truck bed for carrying implements and small engine machines, big towing capacity, four tires in the back and two in the front, and was easy to clean between jobs.

The next piece of equipment purchased was a trailer. At first our idea was to rent a trailer with specifications that would allow towing of plant shipments and a tractor. These trailers have to be outfitted with brakes that match the braking of the truck so that the trailer brakes in tandem with the truck brakes. This helps to keep the trailer from causing an accident or a rollover. Extra chains and hitch locks keep the trailer from breaking away from the truck and sides can be added by a welder. There is no substitute for a safe driver.

We found out very quickly that equipment trailers could not be rented locally, probably because of the liability to the owners and we had to purchase one. Some of the strongest trailers with tandem wheels were available near Lake Okeechobee at the time, so we ordered one from there.

Buy a trailer that has at least two sets of tires. Our first trailer had two sets and the second had three sets because of what we learned. When you are towing a heavy load, particularly at jobsites, you have an excellent chance of picking up nails and other sharp debris. The flat or shredded tire can cause an accident or rollover on the road. Tires have to be continuously checked, but eventually one will go flat. The more tires you have, the greater chance that you will be able to handle the situation safely. You have time to get to the side of the road and call for assistance if necessary. On board replacement tires are an absolute necessity because you can get someone to change these big tires, but you can't count on anyone to have the tire you need. If the repair or replacement takes too much time, the day could be completely wasted in terms of getting any work done. So, buy trailers with as many tires as you can.

Chapter 28

Really Heavy Equipment

Landscapers need a way to move very heavy foliage without getting injured, so front end loaders are very important to have. Companies who own them are very happy to rent them out because they get a premium price for short rentals.

One month we paid $3,000.00 for a rental machine to complete some projects that were large enough to make the rental worthwhile. It was time to buy one because a lot of work was coming in and rental was costing too much.

We rented a number of machines from one local establishment and decided to approach the owner to discuss purchasing one. Unfortunately, the machine we were interested in was sold.

I inquired at a rental place sixty miles north of us and a salesman told me about a big front loader for sale in central Florida that they were interested in moving along. They had taken a model in on trade that was not their regular line and wanted to move it as quickly as possible.

By this time, we had tried out a lot of used equipment and had decided that the words "used" and "good" didn't fit in the same sentence. Contractors generally use up every last motion in these loaders before they let them go. In months of driving these, the flaws were too great to consider paying money for. Repairs and upkeep are very expensive, so you don't dare buy one that is worn out. Because the gentleman sounded sincere, I took a chance and drove to a small Central Florida town, eight hours round trip. I would have never known about it because it wasn't in a local showroom or being advertised. I told my husband I was probably going to look at another awful piece of machinery and we just laughed. He went to work and I headed across the state.

They were ready for me. What I didn't know when I arrived was that the good old boys at the equipment yard had a friend with a farm who used to work with them. He wanted the machine to use on the tree farm he owned.

First they told me that the machine was on a farm and gave me the address. They didn't mention that these were rural roads with no street signs. After driving around for forty five minutes trying to follow the instructions, I went back to the equipment yard to have someone take me there.

Then, they just couldn't let anyone go with me because the floor wasn't covered with enough sales people. I waited for a salesman to come in and finally, we headed to the farm. When we got there, guess what, the tractor was sitting there like a dead thing with the hood up, as if it was in need of repair. The idea was to discourage me or keep me from test driving it. I looked at the salesman and told him that I had been looking for a long time and hadn't made this trip across the state for nothing. I asked him if there was a hotel nearby that I could stay in overnight if they needed more time to get it running, or get a mechanic out to assess the problem. He went over and talked the men into letting me drive the machine. They seemed to reinstall something that would make the starter work and laughed like maniacs.

They gave me instructions, speaking very slowly, and told me to be very careful not to run into anything. It is so funny now that I look back at the whole thing, but that day I was just boiling inside, trying not to let them see how mad I really was. I had become an expert operator of a variety of these machines we rented because there were only three of us and I was needed. It didn't take long to discover that these loaders are not physically hard to use because the hydraulics do all the work. You need to be safety conscious and watch out for other people, but operating these big machines is not rocket science.

Anyway, they stood back, apparently expecting me to crash into something and I put the machine through its paces. This was finally the one we had been looking for, with all the features I needed to do the work. I almost couldn't contain myself I was so happy to find it. It was an articulator that could get into tight places and turn corners around houses to facilitate easy placement of trees. The way the tires run across the ground keeps from tearing up the client's lawn. It could lift at least 4,000 pounds easily and was good for installing sod, tree moving, and general demolition work.

The logistics of the deal were not as straight forward. The machine was on a farm where a bunch of people who hadn't bought it, were using it for heavy work every day. Their buddies wanted them to have it. On top of everything else, they were amused that the boss had sent a woman across the state, someone who wasn't supposed to be a buyer or be able to operate the machine.

It was late in the day so I made an offer and filled out an application for credit. Then I headed for home wondering all the way how this could ever work out. It was tough waiting, but after trying to put the machine in the hands of the hands of their buddy, things didn't turn out. Reluctantly, they called me to set up the final paperwork and sell the machine to me. We had been trying to get something decent for over a year and this was the first articulator that was in really good shape.

They told me to pick it up in a different town (I never knew why) in Central Florida. This second trip was a total waste because when I arrived with a truck and trailer at the second location the machine we were so thrilled to obtain was in the shop with parts all over the floor. At this point, we wondered if they were taking parts off a great machine to use on another one locally. These were very small towns and we were outsiders. Everyone in town was a friend except us. It took a couple of calls to the guy who first told me about the front loader. He made them put it back together and told me that they had to fix something. Of course, the mechanic couldn't do it that day so I could leave with it, and once again, I had to bring back a truck and trailer the next day. It might have helped if my husband could have come but he was busy on another job. The thing is that we were buying an articulating loader for around $15,000.00 that sold for around $40,000.00 and more at the time. The opportunity was so stunning that we couldn't walk away from the deal, no matter how trying they were making things for us.

On the return trip, we had decided that we would not take the machine until I had a chance to once again put it through a series of tests. If I even suspected that they had taken parts from it for some other buddy, or tampered with it in any way, the deal was off. Again, the price I negotiated for the machine was around $15,000.00 and the comparable new ones were in the $40,000.00 range.

They took me seriously this time, and when I got there the second time, the machine looked and worked great. I loaded and chained it to the trailer with the guys looking on like they were at the circus. Why did it have to be like this? I wondered if everyone had gone crazy. Wasn't it enough that we were paying good money for a piece of equipment we needed for a business?

It really was a terrific machine and we made a lot of money with it with very few repairs. We kept it when we changed directions and the business ended. It still came in handy after the hurricanes cleaning up the property.

So, if you can buy new equipment it will be easier than finding a good used machine, but you have to factor the cost into your clients' estimates. Only buy used equipment if you are absolutely sure that it is in excellent condition. Otherwise, the used equipment could cost you more than a new machine over a period of time. Heavy equipment comes with a big price tag in the repair department and huge liability on the jobsite. Even more importantly, it has to be treated with respect even when being towed home. The weight is measured in tons and even a small mistake in traffic can have tragic consequences. Fortunately, we never had an occurrence or accident, but it was close a couple of times.

When you own equipment in any part of the country, it is important to get it off the jobsite at the end of the day because there is a lot of theft of these machines. Apparently, they get huge prices for stolen equipment and some are even shipped overseas. Don't leave anything on a jobsite at night if you can possibly get the equipment out of there.

It takes a lot of patience and fortitude to land a good deal on used equipment because there is little availability, less people are in the business, and very few good ones traded in.

The problem with having to rent machines to do work for customers is that no matter how careful you are to plan a date to do the work, the weather can change during the day. At that point, you are paying hefty bills for a loader and may have to pay again tomorrow if you can't complete the work because of the weather. You might have to forfeit your profits in a situation like this. If you own the machine, coming back is not a problem because there is less of an up charge to you as a contractor.

Another problem you can run into is that the rental department may have so much demand and so few loaders that you simply can't get a machine when you need one. At any rate, I still think it is incredibly important to try out many manufacturers to make sure that you are making a good long term choice for the line of work you are in. We would have made a massive mistake if we had bought the first one we thought was perfect.

No matter what, your mastery of the principles in this book will make it possible to get the competitive edge. It just takes a lot more patience. If you are not patient, send a family member to do the shopping, like my husband did.

Chapter 29

The Keys

Wow! You can't wait to get out and drive your new car. In their excitement to leave, most people forget a couple of critical last steps.

❖ **Do you have all the copies of your paperwork?**

You may need facts listed on these pages for your insurance agent or banker. Don't leave without your copies. If you are applying for a private loan to see if you can obtain a better rate you will need them.

❖ **Do you know the maintenance schedule required by the manufacturer to keep your warranties in force?**

If you do not follow the maintenance guidelines for your vehicle, you might find that standard warranties and even extra warranties that you have included as part of your loan are not in force when you need the wonderful things they promised and you bought.

Imagine your horror when an expensive repair that would have been covered under your warranty is turned down and you have to reach into your bank account and pull out several unexpected hundreds of dollars. You are saying "but, but" and they are saying that it was all in the paperwork they gave you when you signed up for the warranty. Pay close attention and make sure you get a maintenance schedule related to the requirements of the warranty, read it and understand it. Follow it to the letter.

Is the tag on your car? I can't begin to tell you how easy it is to drive down the street and not even realize that you have no tag on the back of your vehicle. You are already exhausted. Do you want to have to explain this to a vigilant policeman? While you might get in some interesting car talk about the new car, he will likely just go ahead and issue you a ticket for driving without one. His city needs revenue.

Don't depend on the salesman to take care of this significant detail without your participation. The car is sold now and his interest in you is waning. There is a new client in his binoculars and you are disappearing into the ether.

When my husband picked up his truck, he called the insurance agent to add it to our policy. Then he drove it to an agent for the new truck inspection. She walked around the truck and when she reached the back bumper, she asked him if he forgot to put the tag on. Luckily, he was very close to where he bought it. I drove him back to get it and we attached it before he got a ticket. He could have driven all over town for days and not known.

❖ Don't leave the parking lot until your salesman goes over the operating features of the car one more time.

When you have been driving another vehicle for a while, you are used to the controls for the wipers, windshield washer, radio, signal lights, emergency signals, brightness knobs, shifters, and other functions. Before you leave the car lot, insist that someone show you one more time where they are and how they work in this car.

How many times have you heard someone say that they once wrecked a brand new car? You can sympathize that such a weird thing could happen and give them a copy this book, because you know they will at least get a better deal the next time.

Why does this happen so often to good drivers? I once saw a customer drive out of the lot onto a crowded road in her new car. She made a left hand turn and thought she was signaling. Instead, she used the windshield cleaner knob. Water shot all over the window as she entered the road. She didn't see another vehicle emerging from across the street right away. They almost collided, but luckily, both got away without injury.

So, please be safe and take the few minutes it takes to have your salesperson go over the important elements of your dashboard before you drive. It can save your new car, your good health, and my peace of mind.

Chapter 30

Transferable Skills

Everything in this book can be used for every transaction you ever make. That is why I suggested in the beginning of The Real Deal-For Smart Car Buyers that cars are only one commodity upon which you will be able to negotiate successfully.

Have you ever watched couples walk into a home and immediately declare that "This is just beautiful!" on some of the popular house shows? Well, they are probably standing in a foyer that has no electric plugs, paint over water damage, and a floor that will have to be replaced soon. It is no different than falling in love with the appearance of a car with flaws. There is no need to give away too much information until the house has been really inspected and critical needs are met. You could wind up paying much more for the house.

Our Current House- I didn't even see the house. The house really didn't matter at all in any way. What grabbed me was the land. Here was a lot that was over a half acre, like a park in the middle of an area that boasts any kind of store nearby, a neighborhood that had grown up house by house, with all the houses different from one another, but well kept. There was no association and no monthly fees. I was secretly in meltdown.

The realtor only wanted to show the house and we didn't talk about the lot, except to treat the yard like it was too much grass to mow. It was actually hard to imagine how we would downsize into the house and after categorizing all the work that would have to be done to make it livable and the expense that would generate, put in a low offer. At the time, money was very tight. We bought the house and gradually fixed the flaws. It cost some money, but today, because of the lot, the house is worth at least eight times what we paid for it. Was it easy to ride out the deal? Absolutely not. It was excruciating hoping that this was the house we could settle into. The first time that our offer was tendered, the realtor said that just the night before, another offer had been made and we had to wait for that to play out. It fell through and then our offer was accepted.

Later, the empty lot next door was for sale right when we didn't have enough money to buy it. Our landscaping business made every month a financial challenge as we tried to pay the bills and get new business. There was never a guarantee that there would be enough money. I had always loved having no neighbor or house on the lot next to ours because it gave us so much privacy and quiet. It was on the market for at least two years before I approached my neighbor. We couldn't imagine why someone had not purchased it. There were some drawbacks, like a lot of work to do to clean it up, but we had the machinery to do it. The owner was looking for a hefty cash down payment (which had driven a lot of buyers away) and when I asked why she needed so much down, told me that she owed big taxes on the lot and her house a couple doors down. Things were out of control. I asked if she would mind if we talked to the tax people to see if there was a way to save her house and buy the lot from her. It would not be long before both properties could be in serious jeopardy. So, we worked things out so that she could keep her property and sell the lot to us. Fortunately, we were able to pay off the land in a lump sum agreement a few years later when things weren't so tight financially. It gave her money to work with in her elder years and stay in her home. It doubled the land at our house and became a financial resource for *our* retirement.

This negotiation was in all our best interests. At the time, someone could have probably paid the tax notes and taken the property lock, stock, and barrel. One of our friends told us that she was asking way too much for the property and we were crazy to buy it. Our stance was that the price was reasonable, we were both younger and still working, and that we could afford it.

So, how does this relate to the spirit of The Real Deal?

Our neighbor had been living next door for over twenty years and had lost her husband. Moving would have been very difficult for her.

On our side of the deal, there was only one shot at keeping the lot from being developed. So, we found a way to make it work for everyone. When we took the fences down to join the property with ours, we made an amazing discovery. There were old lily ponds, made by her husband before he passed on. We fenced them in and restored them so she got to see the lilies bloom again.

We partially paid for the lot by using it to grow and store plants for the landscaping business. The transaction worked out well for all of us. The Real Deal is a fair deal.

The Big Mower Problem-What about the lawn mower for this expanded yard? When I went to buy it, a shipment had just come in with around six riding mowers of this kind in a relatively small shop. The retail price was around two thousand dollars but I asked if it was possible to purchase one of the machines for around 25% less. The gentleman behind the counter laughed at the notion, so I told him I would be glad to sit on the bench and wait until he called the owner and proceeded to sit on the bench. Finally, he took the phone out of the room and called the owner. When he came back, he wanted to know how I would pay for the machine, I handed him a credit card, and we arranged delivery. Why did I get such a whopping discount on a machine? Timing. If you have ever owned your own business, you know that there is nothing as important as cash flow. If you get the delivery of six monster mowers and you have an invoice from the manufacturer coming your way, it makes sense to let a couple of them get out the door for less money, but be ready to pay your supplier. What I am saying is look around yourself for clues everywhere you go to shop for anything. You might pick up information.

Was it easy to sit on a bench and wait for the man behind the counter to make up his mind whether to call his boss? No. This does not come naturally to me or anyone else. But I will not let feeling really uncomfortable get in the way of saving a few hundred dollars on the perfect mower when I know it is possible.

The next mower- It came from a big box store and I still have it. Regularly a couple grand again, it was time for a new one at the worst time of year, summer in Florida. The grass grows so fast that if you don't mow every couple of weeks, you start telling people your house is the one behind the grass. Waiting to get one is not an option on over an acre. At the store, we were looking the mower over and a really nice salesperson came over. I told her it was just what we needed but they were so expensive that I didn't know what we would do and that maybe we should finally cave in and have someone mow for us. Out of the blue, she asked us to come with her. We went out to the lot behind the store and she showed us the same machine with a blue mark on it.

The blue mark meant that the machine was sold new and that the buyer returned it to the store over a deck problem. They had sent the machine back to the manufacturer to be refurbished. The machine could now be purchased for $900.00 with a full warranty. We jumped on it immediately because it was a reputable company and with a full warranty we had no fears. Just by telling her our story and hesitating on a purchase, we saved well over a thousand dollars and the store got rid of the machine that was taking up space.

The Kitchen Kick-off - The power of hesitation cannot be overstated but its use is relative to the situation. I had admired a double oven at another big box store for years. One day, don't ask me why, but the store put a sign on last year's model for less than $800.00. A big double oven, both self-cleaning, and the top one with convection was my personal heaven. I ran to the clerk and found out that there were three in inventory. My husband thought I had gone mad because he thought that was too much to pay and there was no place for it in the house. I remember telling him that I would get it to our place if I had to put it on my back and wear roller skates to get it home. It kicked off building a kitchen with their kit, but saved enough money to help buy other new appliances and cabinetry. We saved a fortune on the kitchen by building it ourselves and were very grateful that it didn't ruin our marriage.

Was it easy? No. The kitchen took a very long time and frayed nerves as we experimented our way through it, but in the end we wound up with something terrific that continues to save money for us every single day.

The refrigerator was from a big box store and after finally deciding what would work, we again hesitated and the salesman found a way to bring the price down and get a better price on an extended warranty.

Every dollar saved is important because none of us know what life will throw at us next. There are even residual savings like the electric bill when you can buy energy efficient appliances.

The bottom line is that all the negotiation skills you can learn from this book apply to just about everything you buy. Will it be easy for you to do every time? No. But over time, if you slow down and give it a try, you will be successful.

What Life Throws At You- You can always use these skills in the "what life throws at you" scenarios. It is important not to accept all situations as absolute. When my sons were in school, we had a couple of events that fell into this category.

My eldest was in junior high school when he was rejected for a spot in the band. He wanted so badly to get in. For some reason, he was not allowed to register and I couldn't get them to admit him.

Then I got the following call one day, "This is the principal's office. Your son is inebriated and has passed out. Come right away and pick him up." I told the caller to call 911, get an ambulance, and have him taken to the nearest ER. I left right away for the school hoping to arrive before the ambulance, terrified that someone had done something to him or that there was a medical condition. The principal assured me that all mothers were defending their children and that this had definitely happened. He offered to drive me to the hospital because I was so shaken. When we arrived at the hospital, I was taken to a room where he was under observation. When he turned his head to see me, I realized that it was not my son at all. It turned out that there were two students in the school with the same first and last name and the secretary pulled my son's records first. It was an honest mistake, but on the way home, the principal, appalled that this had happened, asked "Is there anything we can do for you to show how sorry we are for this incident?" I said, "Actually, there is. My son was devastated about not being allowed to get in the band program and I would appreciate it if you could find a way to get him in. We are just a few days into the year and I know he will do what it takes to catch up."

The next day my son was called to the principal's office, I was there too, and told that they were going to get him into the band because his mother had so much belief in him. He was ecstatic to have a chance and asked when he could start. The same day I started more negotiations on a trombone and making payments as a single mom with little money to spare. He received the highest honor his award winning band had to offer at his high school graduation and went on to become a nuclear power plant operator after serving in the nuclear program in the Navy.

When he arrived at the ninth grade, my youngest son encountered no opposition when joining the band the next year, played the saxophone, and ultimately became a high level networker. Both of them went into the Navy and served for years. They used their time in the Navy to learn the skills they transferred into jobs, along with goals for their future.

The Free Disney Vacation- Once we arrived at school to see my eldest son off on a class trip to Disney World. His little brother was pre-school and wanted to go on the trip too. The bus was held up and I asked why they were waiting to leave because I couldn't stand his little brother's disappointment at not being in the class. He wanted to go with the other kids. It turned out one of the chaperones didn't show up. I offered to chaperone on the spot if they could allow my other little son to come along. Forms were shoved at me to sign and in minutes we were approved. The three of us jumped on the bus and had the time of our lives at the theme park for free.

The Really Mean Teacher Story- When my youngest son began to have a stomach ache one morning before elementary school, I thought he must have come down with something and kept him at home. He improved during the morning. The next day, the same thing happened again and he didn't want to go to school. The doctor could find nothing wrong and said he could go back the next day. On the way home, he started talking about not going back to school anymore. This was all so bizarre that I asked him what was going on in his classroom.

He began telling me that his teacher was making fun of students on a personal level with cruel insults. One girl was being picked on mercilessly and insulted in front of the whole class, often made to cry. He told me that the teacher was giving out odd punishments and everyone was afraid of her.

I got on the phone and called some other mothers I knew and asked if they were hearing the same thing from their children. Several of them told me they were very upset, but fearing that their child would be singled out for more abuse each day, they had not stepped forward. I found five mothers who agreed that there was a big problem. So, we decided to get a meeting with the principal to discuss the children's concerns. The meeting date was set and we hoped to find a solution to the problems.

On the night before the meeting, I called each of the mothers to remind them of our school appointment and to my surprise, every one of them backed out of coming the next morning. I could not persuade them to come forward and tell the stories they were hearing. Without them, I was one person, with one very unhappy little boy, not likely to be paid attention to.

I was self-employed as a wholesaler to the floral trade and had a very tiny business going that allowed me to make some money and be there for my young children. I was a divorced single mother. I had little time to deal with the school and couldn't take off much time from work.

I went to the meeting, hoping that the other parents would show up. Instead of support, I found myself alone, faced by a committee of three administrators, including the Principal.

After going over what we were all hearing about the way the children were being treated and asking what could be done about it, I pointed out that my son was wanting to quit school and that the stress of being in that classroom was weighing so heavily on him that he was having stomach pains in the morning. I let them know that his pediatrician could not find any other reason for the physical distress that he was having.

I mentioned that there were a lot of other mothers who knew about the situation and that they would definitely show up at some point to discuss the problems. I did not want my son to have a negative experience in school that would cause ongoing problems in future years. I asked for him to be transferred to another classroom and another teacher for the balance of the year. It was late afternoon and school was out for the day. The next morning, he was taken to a new classroom where he met with a new teacher who turned out to be the one that ran a respectful class.

I let my son know that this was a one-time opportunity that we were granted to set things right and that he needed to work hard and give the new teacher his very best.

Later, his new teacher said it was the oddest thing because no one told him why his new student was being moved. For all he knew he had been given some unruly kid he was supposed to bring around. Instead, he found that the little guy just wanted to be there and did all his work with no trouble. He said it was as if he wanted to be the best student in his class. There are defining moments in time that have to be recognized as important. Children have to be nurtured and protected. Your negotiation skills can make the critical difference in their lives and help them to develop a sense of fairness.

In the end, it doesn't matter whether you are using your negotiation skills to buy a new vehicle or to advocate for your family. You are in charge of what you spend and how you are treated. You are powerful, no matter who you are or how much money you are spending. Every dollar is important to the businesses you choose to buy from.

So, enjoy life, save money, and get The Real Deal.

Chapter 31

From The Author

I genuinely hope that the information contained in this book will help you to save money, save time, and make your life better than ever.

This book could be invaluable to sons and daughters graduating from high school or college. It will be a good idea to keep a copy around for reference to use in negotiating for any large purchase over the years.

I am sending you out with an army behind you. I hope that you are going to be so good at buying big ticket negotiable items that you will have to give away this book to keep from having to negotiate for your friends, relatives, and acquaintances! No one is a natural, but you can become a natural negotiator and it will be easier and easier as you see the results.

Visit Amazon.com for information about upcoming titles in THE REAL DEAL ® series!

Best Regards!

Linda Balk

www.ingramcontent.com/pod-product-compliance
Lightning Source LLC
Chambersburg PA
CBHW020528290526
45786CB00002B/797